Bird's New Home

by Lori Mortensen
illustrated by Gabriel Alborozo

Bird wanted a new home.

"I need some twigs,"
she said.

Vole came along.

He said, "You don't want twigs. Dig a hole like I do. Holes are very cozy."

"No, thanks," said Bird.

Vole and Bird did not want the same thing.

Fox came along.

Fox said, "You don't want twigs. You don't want a hole. Find a hollow log like I do."

"No, thanks," said Bird.

Fox and Bird did not want the same thing.

Bee came along.

"Make a home with wax like mine," said Bee.

"No, thanks," said Bird.

Bee and Bird did not want the same thing.

Bird got three twigs.
She got six twigs.
She got more twigs!

Bird made her home
from twigs.
It was very high in a tree.

Bird could see all around.
"It's just what I want,"
she said.